DUNBAR BRANCH

DUNBAR BRANCH

FOR SUSAN, BEN AND LULU ∽ J.R.

FOR MY OWN DEAR HERCULES, JOSÉPH BALIT ∽ C.B.

The Twelve Labours of Hercules copyright © Frances Lincoln Limited 1997
Text copyright © James Riordan 1997
The right of James Riordan to be identified as the author of this work
has been asserted by him in accordance with the Copyright, Designs
and Patents Act, 1988 (United Kingdom).
Illustrations copyright © Christina Balit 1997

First published in Great Britain in 1997 by Frances Lincoln Limited,
4 Torriano Mews, Torriano Avenue, London NW5 2RZ

British Library Cataloguing in Publication Data available on request

ISBN 0-7112-1165-5

Designed by Sarah Slack
Set in Stone Serif and Trajan

Printed in Hong Kong
9 8 7 6 5 4 3 2 1

THE TWELVE LABOURS OF
HERCULES

JAMES RIORDAN ✼ CHRISTINA BALIT

FRANCES LINCOLN

Author's Note

⊚⊘

*O*f all the great heroes of the ancient world, the most famous was Hercules. The Greeks called him Herakles, meaning 'Glory to Hera'; the Romans renamed him Hercules. (He is called Hercules in this book because that is the name most people know him by, but the other characters are called by their traditional Greek names.) His superhuman strength, courage and skill won him lasting fame and immortality among the gods on Mount Olympus.

Hercules was set twelve almost impossible tasks, and succeeded in carrying out every single one of them. So extraordinary was his success that, even to this day, we often describe an exceptionally difficult task as 'herculean'.

This is the story of Hercules' life and of the twelve labours that he performed.

∾ CONTENTS ∾

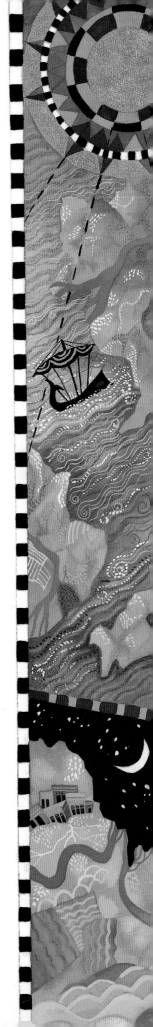

The BIRTH *of* HERCULES 9

The LION *of* NEMEA 14

The HYDRA *of* LERNA 18

The GOLDEN HIND *of* CERYNEIA 22

The WILD BOAR *of* ERYMANTHUS 26

The AUGEAN STABLES 30

The BIRDS *of the* STYMPHALIAN MARSH 32

The WHITE BULL *of* CRETE 36

The WILD MARES *of* DIOMEDES 40

HIPPOLYTE'S GOLDEN BELT 44

KING GERYON'S CATTLE 46

The GOLDEN APPLES *of the* HESPERIDES 50

CERBERUS *the* HOUND *from* HADES 55

The DEATH *of* HERCULES 58

Map 62

The BIRTH of HERCULES

"Hercules - Glory to Hera!" roared great Zeus from Mount Olympus. The father of the gods did a dance for joy, and made the heavens rumble. He had just heard that a son was about to be born to him.

"Hercules - what a fitting name. He will be stronger than a lion, wiser than the stars, a warrior-hero, protector of gods and men. And one day he will save the gods from the race of giants! I swear that this son of mine, descended from Perseus himself, shall be king of Mycenae. Ah, Hercules, my son, my son!"

But Zeus' wife, the goddess Hera, was far from pleased at having Hercules named after her - in fact, she was furious, for the child was not hers! Its mother-to-be was a woman called Alcmene and, with Zeus as its father, the baby would be half-man, half-god.

When she learnt that the baby was to be born the next day, Hera plotted revenge on her unfaithful husband. She asked him sweetly, "Do you swear that the next son born in our family and descended from Perseus will be king of Mycenae?"

"I do!" thundered Zeus.

At once the jealous goddess hurried off to Mycenae, and arranged for Nicippe, the wife of King Sthenelus, who was also descended from Perseus, to give birth to her child an hour before Hercules was born. He was named Eurystheus, and he was Hercules' half-brother.

Zeus could not go back on his word - so now Eurystheus would be king of Mycenae.

But Hera was not satisfied: the green snake of jealousy still writhed within the mother of the gods.

A year later, she sent two deadly serpents with poisoned fangs and strong coils to kill the infant Hercules in his cot. But the serpents were no match for Zeus' baby son. Next morning, servants found the infant sitting up, gurgling and laughing, whirling the dead serpents round his head like skipping ropes. He had tied their heads into a knot and strangled them with his bare hands!

As Hercules grew to manhood, he was taught by the best tutors: Eurytus showed him how to use a bow; Amphitryon, to drive a chariot; Castor, to ride a horse; Pollux, to wrestle; Linus, to sing and play the lyre; and Chiron, the art of healing.

Hercules grew up tall and broad-shouldered, with dark curly hair and a gaze like smouldering fire behind his amber-flecked grey eyes. No youth could match him in wrestling or any other sport; and he often used his strength to help those in need.

For one such deed, the grateful king of Thebes gave Hercules his daughter Megara to be his wife. It was a perfect match: Megara and Hercules were devoted to each other. In time they had three sons. No family could have been happier.

But their happiness was not to last. The vengeful Hera was determined that misery should follow Hercules like a shadow.

One day, she enveloped him in a fit of madness. Not knowing what he was doing, Hercules seized his poor wife and children and threw them into a fire, where they burned to death.

At once his blind rage dissolved like mist, and he was overcome with remorse. What had he done? Why had he killed those he loved most? And how was he to pay for his dreadful crime? Mad with grief, he wept uncontrollably. He fell into a troubled sleep, and in a dream he was told to go to the temple at Delphi and accept whatever judgement the Oracle should decree.

Hercules walked barefoot across the rocky land for many days, until he arrived at Delphi. There, at the top of a steep cliff, stood the famous temple. He climbed the jagged rock and entered the temple, torn and bleeding, then fell upon his knees before the altar and sobbed out his tale of woe.

"Tell me how I may cleanse myself of this evil," he cried.

There was a long silence. Then the voice of the priestess echoed round the walls and marble columns.

"Go to the city of Mycenae. There you must serve your half-brother, King Eurystheus, for twelve years. He will set you twelve tasks, each harder than the one before. If you perform these labours successfully, your soul will find peace."

The Oracle had spoken.

The labours of Hercules were about to begin.

The LION
of NEMEA

For as long as he had been king, Eurystheus feared that one day Hercules would try to take away his throne, so he was less than pleased when his half-brother arrived at his gate. But when he learned that the Oracle had put Hercules at his mercy, he rubbed his hands in glee: Hercules' first task, he decided, would also be his last.

Summoning his half-brother, he said to him, "Hercules, a savage lion is terrorising the countryside of Nemea, near Corinth. The beast comes down from the hills at night, killing shepherds and their sheep. Your first task is to slay the lion and bring me its skin as proof that it is dead."

The king knew, though Hercules did not, that no weapon could pierce the lion's hide.

Hercules set out for the valley of Nemea, taking with him a strong net, a spear and his favourite club carved from a wild olive tree. It was early morning when he caught sight of the lion returning to its hillside lair. He settled down behind a rock to wait.

It was not long before the beast came over the brow of a hill, its great jaws dripping blood. The very sight of the massive beast would have sent most men fleeing in terror, but not Hercules. He leapt out as the monster passed and aimed his spear.

The spear whistled through the air straight and true, hitting its target with a jarring thud - and bounced harmlessly off the lion's chest as if from solid rock.

The beast turned, snarling with rage, and charged Hercules with a roar, its sharp teeth ready to tear him apart. But Hercules stood his ground. He stretched up and swung the club with all his might. It caught the beast a hefty blow that would have killed any other creature. But the lion was not even stunned; it turned before Hercules could follow up the blow and slunk off to the safety of its den. He pursued it into the cave and tied his net across the entrance so that it could not escape.

Then a terrible fight began: Hercules, with his bare hands, fought the huge lion with its razor-sharp teeth and claws. Gradually he forced the beast back into the net, where it twisted and roared, unable to escape from the cave. The ground trembled as the two wrestled to the death.

Finally, Hercules gained a grip on the lion's throat and choked its breath away.

When he went to skin the carcass, he found that his spear would not pierce its hide. Then he had an idea: using one of the lion's sharp curved claws, he cut through the hide with ease and skinned the shaggy beast.

Hercules returned to the king wearing the lion-skin over his shoulders, its head serving as a helmet. When Eurystheus saw him, the poor man fainted; he thought that the lion had killed Hercules and had now come to tear him limb from limb!

Eventually the king realised it was Hercules in the lion-skin, laughing heartily, and shouted, "You won't live to play tricks on me again!"

The HYDRA
of LERNA

Eurystheus was eager to get rid of Hercules, and wondered what task he should set him next. Suddenly he remembered that at Lerna, not far from Argos, lived the Hydra, a snake-like monster with nine serpent heads. It preyed on passers-by, poisoning them with its deadly fangs and crushing them in its coils. Its breath alone brought death to anyone who ventured near. Many a warrior had tried to slay it, but all had failed. Once they cut off one head, another, even bigger, grew in its place.

Calling Hercules to him, the king said, "Brother, your second task is to slay the Hydra that lurks in the steaming swamps of Lerna."

So Hercules set off towards the Hydra's lair in a chariot driven by his nephew Iolaus. He wore his Nemean lion-skin for protection, and carried a sword and bow.

A cold wind wailed across the bleak marshes, bending the tall, brown-topped bulrushes. When the chariot could go no farther, Iolaus pointed to a distant pool amidst a grove of plane trees.

"Hercules," he said, "you'll find the Hydra there."

Hercules strode forward and waded into the water until it reached his armpits. Now he could see the monster writhing and splashing; but an impassable bog separated him from the beast. All he could do was fire burning arrows high into the air. They fell hissing into the waters of the pool; clouds of steam rose up, and the enraged serpent came slithering towards him, forked tongues flicking out from all its jaws and bloodshot eyes glinting from every socket of its head.

Hercules was not afraid. He stepped forward, holding his breath against the poisonous fumes, and struck out with his sword, slicing off the darting heads one by one. Yet the moment one head flew through the air, another grew in its place. Again and again he slashed off a head - and again and again the heads grew back.

18

By now, the monster had coiled itself about his waist and he could not break free. His great strength began to ebb away as the poison took hold.

Then two huge crabs came crawling out of the mud and locked his ankles in a pincer grip. Any ordinary man would have been crushed to death, his anklebones cracked in two. Not Hercules. He raised his foot and stamped so hard on each crab that their shells smashed to smithereens. But he could not break free of the Hydra's coils, and he was tiring fast.

In desperation, he called Iolaus to his aid.

"Quick, light a fire and bring a torch!" he yelled. Iolaus did as he was bid. Then, as Hercules cut off one head, Iolaus burned its bloody stump, so that no more heads could grow. One by one they destroyed the monster's heads. Now it was the Hydra's turn to tire.

Finally, with a mighty sweep of his sword, Hercules severed the last remaining head and Iolaus burned its stump in the sizzling fire. The evil red gleam of the Hydra's eyes died out. Hercules had slain the Hydra.

He dipped his arrow heads into its poison to make them deadly, then buried the Hydra's body deep in the ground, and returned safely with Iolaus to Mycenae.

"It is done. I have killed the Hydra," he told the king. And he described how he had done the deed.

But Eurystheus shook his head.

"No, no, I cannot count this as a labour," he said. "You were helped by Iolaus."

Only when Hercules threatened to dig up the Hydra's body and drag it to Mycenae, did the king reluctantly accept that Hercules had passed his second test.

The GOLDEN HIND
of CERYNEIA

"If I cannot rid myself of Hercules in a feat of strength," Eurystheus said to himself, "I'll have him killed while he's out hunting. I'll send him to capture the Golden Hind. It is protected by the goddess Artemis, and she has vowed to kill any man who steals her sacred deer. No mortal can outwit the gods."

The story goes that when the goddess of hunting was a child, she had spotted five deer grazing on the banks of the dark-pebbled River Celadon; they were bigger than bulls, with golden horns and bright bronzed hoofs.

Racing after them, swift-footed Artemis caught four with her own hands and harnessed them to her chariot. But the fifth escaped into the Ceryneian Hills near Arcadia, and ever since, the goddess had given it her divine protection.

Hercules set off across Peloponnesus, and for a whole year stalked his prey. As spring turned to summer, autumn to winter, he pursued the creature over marsh and plain. With the passing of the months, it seemed that the hind's speed and guile would save it from Hercules, just as it had from Artemis.

Then, as the spring narcissus bloomed again, the animal began to tire. One day, Hercules glimpsed the hind's horns flashing in the sunlight as it raced up a distant hill. The sight heartened him and, as the weary deer came down to drink at the River Ladon, he took careful aim and fired his bow. The arrow passed between bone and sinew, not even drawing blood, but pinning the hind's forelegs together. He had captured the Golden Hind!

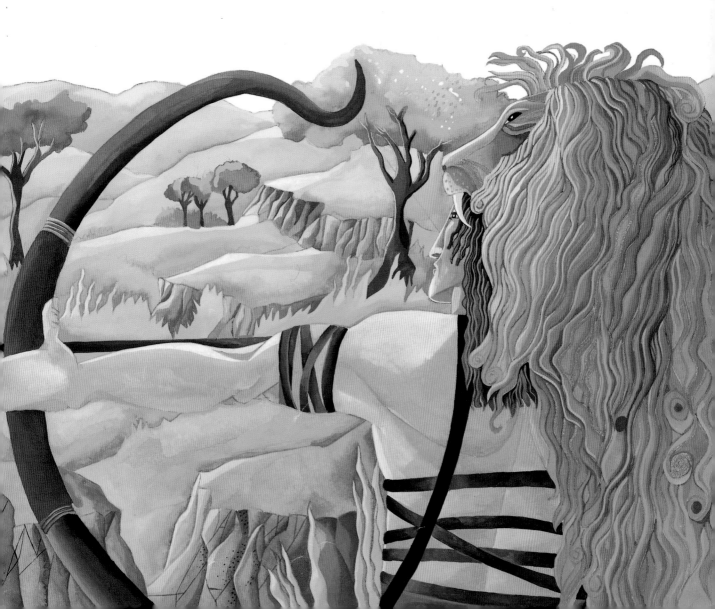

As he was walking back, the trophy slung over his shoulder, he suddenly found his path blocked by a tall, graceful woman carrying a bow and quiver.

"Halt!" she cried. "How dare you steal my hind. If you have drawn blood, you shall die."

At once Hercules realised that this must be Artemis, the goddess of hunting. He bowed and quickly explained his mission, but promised to return the hind unharmed after he had shown it to the king.

"I fired an arrow that drew no blood," he said, showing her the hind's legs. So impressed was Artemis with Hercules' hunting skills that she let him go.

"But make sure you return the deer," she said, "or I shall strike you down."

Hercules went safely on his way, his third labour done. And when he had shown the Golden Hind to the astonished king, he kept his word and returned the animal to Artemis.

The WILD BOAR
of ERYMANTHUS

Eurystheus racked his brains to think of an impossible task for Hercules. Then one day, as if from heaven, news arrived of a gigantic wild boar with tusks as long as spears; for months it had been attacking farmers on the cypress-covered slopes of Mount Erymanthus.

"I'll tell Hercules to bring it back here," thought the king. "No one has managed to kill the beast, let alone take it alive."

To Hercules he said, "You did well to capture the Golden Hind. Now, when you have rested, you can go in search of the Wild Boar of Erymanthus."

"I need no rest," replied Hercules. "The hind hunt was but a light exercise to prepare me for future deeds." Then, armed with a trusty club and poisoned arrows, Hercules set off on his quest.

Along the way, he came upon the Centaurs - creatures with the bodies of horses and the heads and shoulders of men. He was glad to rest a while in the company of their chief, Chiron, for it was Chiron who had taught him the art of healing when he was a boy. So the Centaur-chief entertained him with wine left by the god Dionysus four generations earlier. But some of the Centaurs grew drunk on the heady wine and picked a fight with Hercules, attacking him with clubs and rocks. To scare them off, he fired his poisoned arrows into the air. But one accidentally pierced Chiron's knee, and Hercules' old tutor died in agony from the poisoned shaft.

Bitterly mourning the fate of noble Chiron, Hercules continued his journey. He had many other adventures before he reached the foothills of Mount Erymanthus and picked up the boar's trail; its hoofmarks lay deep in the fresh snow and he had no trouble following them up the mountainside.

With his sword gripped tightly in one hand and his stout club in the other, Hercules trod warily along the track until he heard a fierce snorting coming from a clump of bushes - and suddenly a snout poked through the branches, and there before him was the great beast!

In that instant, Hercules noticed that beyond the bushes lay a deep snow-filled hollow. He let out an ear-shattering roar, which scared the boar so badly that it turned tail and fled, stumbling straight into the snowdrift. In no time it was floundering helplessly in the snow and Hercules was able to bind it fast with ropes, heave it upon to his shoulders and carry it back to Mycenae.

When the king caught sight of the monster's sharp tusks and bristling mane, he took refuge inside a big bronze urn and would not come out. He cowered there for days until a servant came and shouted into the urn, "Sire, you can come out now. The beast is dead and its tusks lie in the temple of Apollo at Cumae."

Eurystheus emerged to find that Hercules had grown tired of waiting for his next task; he had gone off to join Jason and his Argonauts on their voyage to Colchis, in search of the Golden Fleece.

The AUGEAN STABLES

Eurystheus was furious that Hercules had caught the wild boar so easily. And when Hercules returned from Colchis, the king had thought up yet another impossible task: to clean out the stables of King Augeas in a single day.

It sounded simple enough. Augeas, king of Elis, was the wealthiest cattle-owner on earth, with countless sheep and cows, as well as three hundred black bulls, two hundred red bulls and a dozen silver-white bulls to guard his herds against marauding beasts. But the king was lazy, and had not cleaned his stables for many years. The stable yards and the surrounding pastures lay knee-deep in dung and, as a result, plague was spreading through the land.

Hercules had no need to ask the way; when he was within fifty miles of the stables he smelt the stench. Holding his nose, he went straight to King Augeas and vowed to clean the yards, folds and pastures by nightfall.

Hearing this, the king roared with laughter.

"It will take you all day to remove one barrow-load," he said. "And it will take a thousand barrow-loads to clean one stable. I'll wager half my fields it can't be done."

Hercules smiled: he had a plan.

First, he knocked two holes in the farmyard walls; then, using every bit of his strength, he built a dam and diverted two nearby rivers, the Peneus and the Alpheus, into the stable yard. As the swirling waters of the two rivers rushed through the yards and stables, they swept all the dung before them out to sea. A few hours later, the stables were clean and sweet-smelling once more.

But the wily King Augeas refused to pay his wager to Hercules. "It was the river gods, not you, who did the work," he cried. "And besides, you were only carrying out the command of Eurystheus."

"In that case," said Hercules, his eyes twinkling, "tell your river gods to cart a thousand barrow-loads of earth back from the dam to send the rivers on their proper course. I shall not do it for you!"

And off he went to Mycenae, to discover what his sixth task would be.

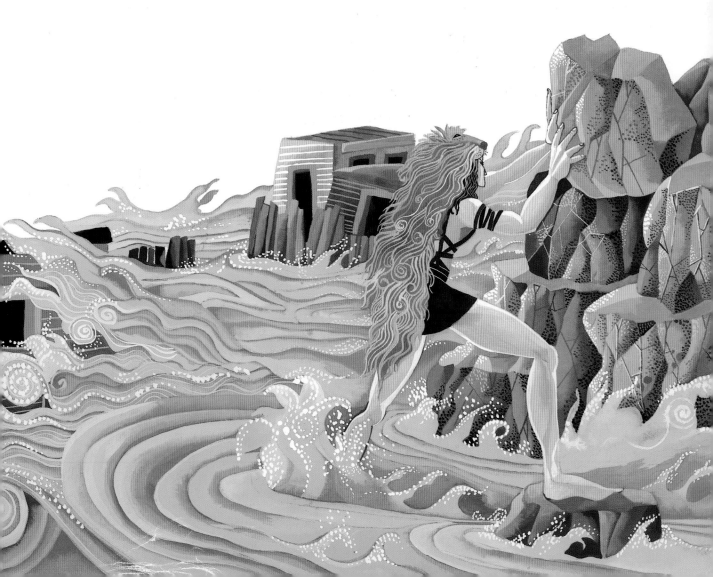

The BIRDS of the STYMPHALIAN MARSH

While Hercules was away in the kingdom of Augeas, King Eurystheus' most skilful archers were out hunting the terrible man-eating birds of the Stymphalian Marsh; their nests lay in the shadow of Mount Cyllene, in Peloponnesus.

These fearsome birds had wings, beaks and claws of brass. They took to the air in huge black flocks, dropping showers of arrow-head feathers from their wings. Once the deadly feathers had pierced the skulls of their defenceless prey below, the birds would swoop down to devour the human flesh. Because of the shifting, boggy ground, no man could get within range of the creatures.

"Surely not even Hercules could rid the land of these birds," thought the king, as he watched his archers returning empty-handed.

When Eurystheus told Hercules of his next task, the hero set off cheerfully, his bow and arrows slung across his back, and journeyed in search of the birds. At the foot of Mount Cyllene, he pushed his way warily through the reeds toward the birds; but he soon found himself sinking into the marsh.

At that moment Athene, goddess of wisdom, happened to pass by. She knew that Hercules was Zeus' favourite son, and decided to help him.

She gave Hercules a huge brass rattle.

"Climb to the top of that crag," she said, "and whirl this rattle with all your might. It makes a noise like the crackling of a forest fire, and will put the birds to flight."

Hercules thanked her and took the rattle. He climbed up the steep crag and when he reached the top, gazed down at the lake below: there, wading in the marsh, were the terrible flesh-eating birds.

Standing on the summit, his arms outstretched, Hercules whirled the rattle round and round above his head; the sound was deafening, as if the skies were tumbling down.

Startled, the birds fluttered up from the marsh. Squawking and screeching, they wheeled about in panic, then flew straight over the crag towards the sun. Hercules fired arrow after arrow into the air, shooting down as many birds as he could. But the rest of the flock passed overhead in a thick black cloud and disappeared from view.

Hercules camped on the mountain top for several days in case the birds returned. But they had left Greece for good, and had flown away to the Isle of Ares in the Black Sea, where they were later spotted by the Argonauts.

Hercules journeyed triumphantly back to Mycenae. Once more, the king had been foiled.

The WHITE BULL
of CRETE

King Eurystheus had heard terrible stories of a fire-breathing bull
running wild on the island of Crete. It was said to be rooting up crops,
knocking down orchard walls and goring anyone who blocked its way.

The white bull had first come from the sea as a gift from the sea-god
Poseidon to King Minos of Crete. Poseidon told the king to make a sacrifice
of the magnificent beast. But Minos, instead of slaying the animal, kept
it for himself and sacrificed another in its place. Angered by the king's
defiance, Poseidon drove the bull mad, and now it was spreading terror
across the land.

It was this bull which fathered the Minotaur, a monstrous creature,
half-man, half-bull, that roamed the centre of the labyrinth at Knossos
and demanded human sacrifices each year. The Minotaur was later killed
by the hero Theseus.

King Eurystheus ordered Hercules to go out and capture the White
Bull of Crete. "After all," thought the king, "the bull is under Poseidon's
command, so no mortal can possibly subdue it."

When Hercules sailed into Crete, King Minos was there to welcome him to his palace.

"No Cretan can venture out of Knossos," the king told him. "Our fields and crops lie in ruins; we will starve to death unless the beast is caught. My army will help you in your task."

"I prefer my own strength and skill to that of any army," replied Hercules, and he set out to seek the wild bull.

He was making his way along a rough path when suddenly, he felt the ground shudder beneath his feet - and there was the white bull, charging him in a frenzy! Hercules leapt aside just in time.

Now he had to think quickly. Before the bull could turn and charge again, he jumped up on to its back, seized its horns and wrestled it to the ground. Then he bound its legs, hoisted it upon his broad back and carried it to his ship. Singlehanded, he had conquered the savage beast.

When King Minos heard the story, he could not thank Hercules enough.
Then he bade him farewell, and the hero sailed home with his prize.

Back at Mycenae, Hercules bore the huge beast to King Eurystheus -
who was too fearful of Poseidon's wrath to have it slaughtered. Instead,
he dedicated it to Hera and set it loose upon the plain of Marathon, near
Athens. So the white bull began a new reign of terror, creating havoc and
ruining crops, until finally the hero Theseus destroyed it.

The WILD MARES *of* DIOMEDES

For Hercules' eighth task, King Eurystheus made a pact with Diomedes of Thrace, King of the Bistones: together they would ensure that Hercules did not return home alive.

King Diomedes was a cruel man, and he had reared four mares to be as savage as himself. He would harness the horses to his war chariot before going into battle and, when he had put his enemies to flight, he would let them loose to feed off the corpses on the battlefield.

The mares had developed such a taste for human flesh that they would eat nothing else. So when there were no wars to provide fodder for his horses, Diomedes would invite guests to his palace; then, while they were sleeping, he would slit their throats and have their bodies thrown to the hungry mares.

"Since you have such a way with animals, Hercules," said Eurystheus, "go to my good friend King Diomedes of Thrace and tame his four mares. It is a simple enough task, dear brother."

Hercules knew that he would not be able to carry out the labour on his own, so he took with him a companion, Abderus. Together they sailed up through the Aegean Sea to the Thracian coast; from there, they went overland to the capital, Tirida, where they were warmly welcomed by King Diomedes. But Hercules was on his guard, for he knew what to expect.

The next day, at dawn - and before the guards could slit their throats - Hercules and Abderus rose from their beds and crept quietly out of the palace chamber. Then, like silent shadows, they stole down to the stables, where they quickly overpowered the grooms.

Now came the hardest part of all. The four mares were fettered with iron chains to brass mangers: Hercules would have to break their chains. Already the mares were neighing restlessly, sensing danger. He would have to act swiftly, before they woke up the palace guard.

With one mighty blow of his sword he cut through the iron chains, and together he and Abderus drove the mares out, trailing their chains behind them. But the horses made enough noise to wake the dead, and Diomedes and his army were soon in pursuit.

They reached the sea-shore, and Hercules left the horses with Abderus while he went back to face Diomedes. Then, before the army was upon him, he cut a channel between them and himself, flooding the low-lying plain so that there could be no escape: Diomedes and his men were drowned in the rushing tide.

But when Hercules went back to rejoin his companion, a terrible sight greeted him. The mares had kicked Abderus to death and were feeding off his flesh!

Hercules' anguish soon turned to rage. He dragged Diomedes' body from the sea and tossed it to the mares, who greedily tore it limb from limb. So Diomedes was served as he had served others.

Now that they had feasted, the mares' hunger was satisfied. Hercules bound their jaws tightly with strong ropes and drove them back to his ship for the journey home. But before setting sail, he named the place Abdera, in memory of his faithful companion.

Once again, King Eurystheus was foiled. When Hercules presented him with the four savage mares, their jaws trussed up with ropes, he hastily had them killed - in case they made a meal out of him!

HIPPOLYTE'S GOLDEN BELT

One day, King Eurystheus' daughter, the princess Admete, came to her father with a strange request. She was soon to celebrate her eighteenth birthday and she had heard there was nothing that Hercules could not do.

"Father," she said sweetly, "for my birthday I would like Hippolyte's golden belt - the one the war-god Ares gave her. Do you think Hercules would fetch it for me?"

A broad smile spread over the king's face.

Hippolyte was Queen of the Amazons, a race of warrior women from Cappadocia who fought wars and ruled their realm while their menfolk cleaned and cooked and brought up the children. When girl-children were born, their mothers trained them in the arts of war; but boy-children were either killed or brought up to do household chores. So skilful were the Amazon warriors that they had defeated every tribe around the Black Sea shores. Never had there been a stronger army.

What a perfect task for Hercules! If he failed, Eurystheus would be rid of him; if he succeeded, he would bring back a splendid birthday gift for Admete.

Accompanied by several Greek warriors, Hercules set sail for the Amazon port of Thermodon, on the Black Sea. He had no desire to engage the fierce Amazons in battle, so he told Queen Hippolyte that he had come in peace to ask for her golden belt as a gift for Princess Admete. The queen, much impressed by the strong, handsome hero, offered him the belt as a token of her respect and trust.

At this point, however, the goddess Hera intervened once more. Disguising herself as an Amazon, Hera spread a rumour among the women that Hercules had come to carry off their queen. When they heard this, a band of Amazons rode out to attack Hercules' men; and the hero, convinced that Hippolyte had played him false, killed her.

The Greeks managed to sail away to safety, taking with them the golden belt, but they were in sombre mood. They had not wished to fight and they knew that Hippolyte had been unjustly killed. A cloud of gloom hung over them. So Hercules delivered the golden belt to Admete, but he never revealed its tragic tale.

KING GERYON'S CATTLE

King Eurystheus was now thoroughly tired of his unwelcome guest, and he hoped to be rid of him by sending him off on a tenth mission: to bring back King Geryon's herd of cattle. Geryon, king of the province of Tartessus on the Spanish peninsular, was a ferocious giant with three heads and bodies resting on two legs. His castle stood on the fabled red land of Erythia - so called because it basked in the rays of the setting sun. His cattle were red too, and were guarded by Eurytion the herdsman and his two-headed watchdog Orthrus.

Hercules had been warned that the sea around Erythia was scalding hot, and that if he tried to reach the island by ordinary ship, the wooden planks would buckle in the heat. While he was considering the problem, he had a stroke of luck: Apollo the sun god offered to lend him his own golden galleon in which he sailed across the sky each day.

Hercules' voyage was full of adventure. Sailing westward out of the Mediterranean, he found his way blocked by a solid wall of rock towering above his ship. It was only by thrusting two cliffs apart that he was able to pass through the narrow straits separating Europe from Africa, now known as the Straits of Gibraltar. To show that he had sailed that way, Hercules built two tall pillars of rock, one on each continent, and to this day they are known as the Pillars of Hercules.

He travelled up to Tartessus and on to the island of Erythia, where King Geryon's cattle grazed.

It did not take him long to find and kill the herdsman and his two-headed hound. He was just driving away the herd when King Geryon himself appeared, saw what was happening and rushed to kill him. Hercules slipped behind a rock and waited until the king was level with the rock. Then he fired an arrow from the side so that it pierced all three heads at once. Geryon fell dead to the ground; and from his red blood sprang the wild cherry tree.

Hercules had great difficulty driving the cattle safely home. As he passed through Italy, the giant Cacus stole two of his finest bulls while he slept; Cacus dragged them backwards by their tails into his cave so as to leave no trace of the theft. But at dawn next day, while Hercules was searching for the lost bulls, he heard their lowing as he passed the giant's cave; so he slew the robber giant and rescued his bulls.

Next, the vengeful Hera sent a swarm of gadflies to bite the cattle and drive them mad, so that they rushed blindly into the River Strymon to avoid being stung. Hercules only managed to rescue them by hurling rocks into the water and forming a path back to dry land - known from then on as the Stepping Stones of Hercules.

Eventually he brought the cattle home to Eurystheus - whose only thanks was to sacrifice the entire herd to Hera!

By now, eight years and a month had passed, and Hercules had performed ten tasks set by the king. But ahead lay the two most difficult tests of all.

The
GOLDEN APPLES
of the HESPERIDES

Eurystheus now commanded Hercules to fetch the golden apples growing in the garden of the Hesperides - a task, he thought, that was surely beyond him.

The apple tree was said to be guarded by a sleepless hundred-headed dragon called Ladon, whose coils wound around its trunk. Zeus had given the tree to Hera as a wedding gift - and nobody, least of all Hercules, could expect to steal from Hera and survive. What is more, no mortal knew exactly where the apples grew; they were said to be tended by three nymphs called the Hesperides, daughters of Atlas, one of the Titans. Only the Hesperides could pick apples from the tree.

Hercules wandered through many lands trying to discover where the tree was to be found. One day, walking along the sea-shore, he came upon some water nymphs. They were Nereids - daughters of Nereus, the Old Man of the Sea.

"Gentle nymphs," said Hercules, "can you tell me where the Hesperides guard the golden apple tree?"

"No," they replied in chorus, "but our father can. Beware, though: when you find him, you must hold him tight, for he will change shape to escape you."

Farther along the beach, Hercules came upon Nereus lying asleep under a covering of seaweed.

When he found himself in Hercules' powerful grasp, Nereus twisted this way and that, unable to escape. All at once, he changed himself into sea-water - but Hercules held on tight, clenching his fists to stop the water running through his fingers. Next, Nereus became a fiery flame that scorched and burned his captor's hands - but still Hercules clung on, despite the pain. Then Nereus changed into a raging lion that would have torn an ordinary man to pieces. Not Hercules. After a fierce struggle, he got the better of the beast, and was choking it - when Nereus suddenly gave up the struggle and took on his own shape once more.

In answer to Hercules' question, Nereus told him, "The garden of the Hesperides lies on the slopes of Mount Atlas, in the province of Mauretania, in Africa. First, you must slay the dragon that guards the tree. But do not pick the fruit yourself. Seek out the giant Atlas, and he will ask his daughters to fetch the apples for you."

So Hercules travelled on, across searing plains and rocky hills, steamy marshes and snowy wastes to Mauretania.

At last, on the lower slopes of Mount Atlas, he found the orchard. The moment he set foot in it, the hundred-headed dragon rushed out at him and would surely have crushed him in its coils. But a single poisoned arrow from the hero's bow put paid to the beast.

Hercules continued on up the mountain until, at the very summit, he saw the giant Atlas, condemned forever to bear the earth upon his back.

When Hercules asked for his help, Atlas readily agreed to have his daughters pick the apples. "But," he added, "you must hold up the world for me while I go to find them."

So Hercules took the world on his shoulders, while Atlas set off down the mountainside, returning soon after with the precious fruit.

Hercules was impatient to be on his way, but Atlas had no wish to give up his newfound freedom, and the longer Hercules shouldered the Titan's load, the more reluctant Atlas was to take it back. Hercules realised he would have to outsmart the giant.

"Atlas," he said, "I fear the globe is badly balanced on my back. Hold it for just a moment, while I make myself more comfortable, then I'll be able to hold it safely."

As Atlas crouched down to take the weight, Hercules stood up, breathed a sigh of relief, and hurried off with his basket of fruit.

"Come back!" cried Atlas. But Hercules did not stop to give him a backward glance.

Hercules carried the apples to King Eurystheus - who was so nervous of Hera's anger that he handed them straight back.

"Return them to the Hesperides," he said, "before Hera discovers they are gone!"

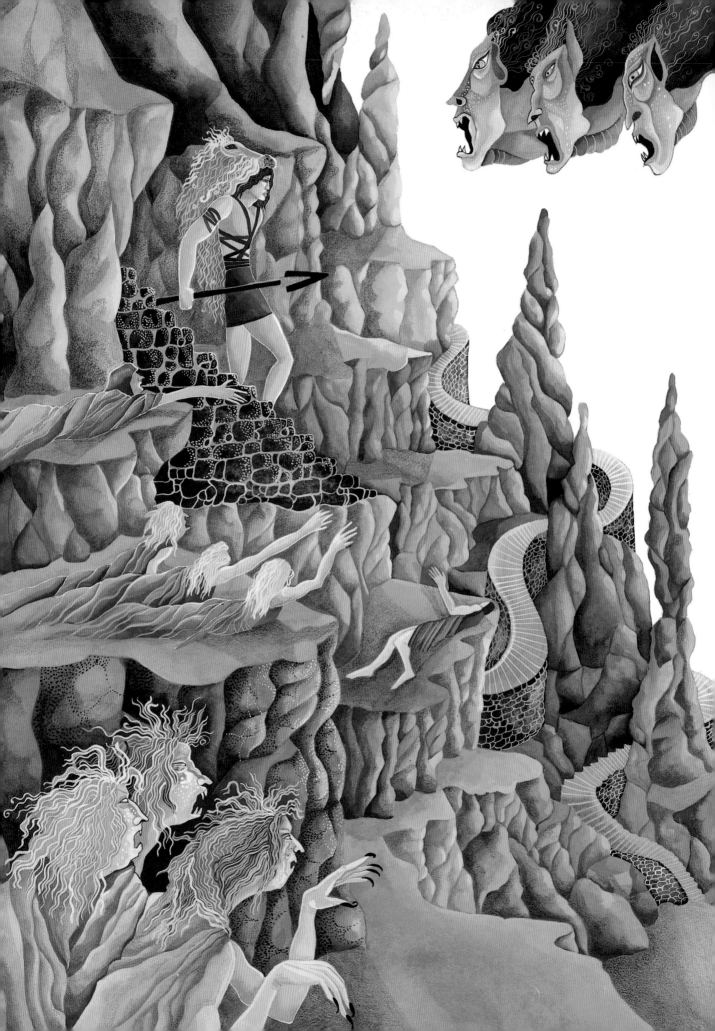

CERBERUS *the* HOUND *from* HADES

Hercules had performed eleven tasks successfully. King Eurystheus now had one last chance to dispose of him.

The king thought long and hard. Then, from the back of his mind came an idea so terrible that he hardly dared speak it aloud.

"Go down to the Underworld," he said, "and bring back Cerberus, the Hound of Hell."

The god Hermes guided Hercules to a cave at Cape Taenarum, near Sparta. From there, Hercules descended by dark, winding paths into the bowels of the earth. He walked swiftly between silent ranks of dead bodies that stretched out their arms towards him; he passed the three cruel Fates holding in their hands the threads of human life, and the three merciless Furies screaming vengeance on all wrongdoers.

He did not stop until he came to the black, swirling waters of the River Styx. Reluctantly, Charon the boatman ferried him across; and after many adventures, he arrived at the gloomy underground palace of King Hades and his wife Persephone.

Quickly, for he did not wish to linger, Hercules told them why he had come. Hades listened grimly, then said, "Take the hound. He is yours - if you can overcome him with your bare hands."

Hercules promised to return Cerberus to Hades once his task was done. Then he made his way back to the gates of Hell, where the terrible watchdog sat, snarling and howling from all three of its throats. Poison dripped from its jaws, its tail lashed the air with a scorpion's sting, and its six bloodshot eyes watched Hercules' every move.

Suddenly, without warning, the hound sprang at his throat. But Hercules was ready: snatching the lion-skin from his back, he threw it over the snarling heads, entangling them in its tough folds. Then he seized the beast in an iron grip, swung it up over his shoulder and bore it off, whining and struggling.

So Hercules entered Mycenae in triumph, his final test completed. He strode into the palace and set Cerberus down before the king.

This was too much for Eurystheus. It was bad enough that Hercules had completed all twelve labours. But now, at the sight of the Hound from Hell, he fled, howling, from the palace and was never seen again.

Hercules took Cerberus quickly back to Hades and returned to the upper world with a light heart. At long last his labours were over. He had atoned for killing his wife and sons. Now he was free and at peace with himself.

The DEATH of HERCULES

It was time for Hercules to leave Mycenae and seek adventures elsewhere.

Hearing that Eurytus, King of Oechalia, in Thessaly, was offering his lovely daughter Iole in marriage to any man who could outshoot him and his three sons, Hercules at once took up the challenge. He won the contest with ease, but Eurytus, fearing Hercules might treat the princess as he had his first wife and children, refused to give her up.

Driven into a frenzy by Hera, Hercules threw himself on the king and his sons, and during the struggle the king's youngest son, Iphitus, was thrown from the palace tower to his death - even though the lad had taken Hercules' side.

So once more, Hercules had brought about the death of an innocent person. In despair, he set off to the Oracle of Delphi to hear his fate. This time, his punishment was to serve Omphale, queen of Lydia, for three years. The queen soon discovered what a strong, and able slave she owned. Hercules helped her rid the kingdom of robbers and wild beasts as easily as another man might carry wood or water.

When his three years of servitude had passed, he set off for home and, after many adventures, reached Calydon in Aetolia. There he fell in love with the beautiful Deianeira, daughter of King Oeneus, and soon they were married.

Some time later, while Hercules was travelling with his wife, they came to the River Evenus, then in full flood. On the bank stood the Centaur Nessus, who offered to carry Deianeira across the river on his back. So, while Hercules waded and swam across, Nessus bore Deianeira to the other bank. But the Centaur then tried to run off with her.

Scrambling on to the bank, Hercules snatched up his bow and shot an arrow which pierced Nessus through the heart.

As the Centaur lay dying, he told Deianeira to take some of his blood and keep it as a charm to preserve her husband's love forever. "Some day you may need such a charm," he whispered with his final breath.

Soon afterwards, Hercules resolved to take his revenge on King Eurytus for the sad death of Iphitus: taking with him a band of warriors, he killed the king, sacked his city and took his daughter Iole captive.

In honour of his victory, Hercules decided to make a sacrifice of a dozen bulls, and despatched a messenger to ask his wife to send him his white ceremonial robe.

Deianeira was jealous of the lovely Iole, and resolved to use the charm Nessus had given her as a way of ensuring her husband's love. She smeared the hem of Hercules' white robe with some of the Centaur's blood before sending it to him. But Nessus had lied about the charm: the blood contained a deadly poison!

As soon as the robe grew warm on Hercules' body, the poison began its work. Hercules writhed in agony. He tried to tear off the robe, but it stuck fast to his flesh and pieces of burning skin peeled off with it. He plunged into a nearby stream, but there his blood hissed and bubbled like molten metal in a vat.

When she heard the dreadful news, Deianeira was filled with remorse. She lay down on their marriage bed, plunged a knife into her breast, and so died.

At Hercules' request, his son Hyllus carried his dying father up to the summit of Mount Oeta and ordered a funeral pyre was built. When the pyre was ready, Hercules calmly lay upon it, his head resting on his club, and his lion-skin spread over him. Then he commanded that the pyre be lit.

As the flames took hold, Zeus gazed down from Mount Olympus and declared, "Only his mother's mortal part shall die. As a snake sheds its skin, so my son shall leave behind his earthly form and rise to join us on Olympus. Hail and welcome, Hercules, my son!" And so, wrapped in a cloud and driven in Zeus' four-horse chariot, Hercules entered Olympus amid peals of thunder and flashes of lightning.

The gods welcomed him warmly. Even Hera, now that he was a god, greeted him as her own son and gave him her young daughter Hebe, goddess of youth, in marriage.

With Hercules' death, Earth suffered a heavy loss, and Atlas' weight felt lighter. But Zeus gained an immortal son of whom he could be justly proud - the glory of Hera and the saviour of the gods!

⚙ MAP ⚙

The TWELVE LABOURS *of* HERCULES

 The LION *of* NEMEA

 The HYDRA *of* LERNA

 The GOLDEN HIND *of* CERYNEIA

 The WILD BOAR *of* ERYMANTHUS

 The AUGEAN STABLES

 *The* BIRDS *of the* STYMPHALIAN MARSH

 The WHITE BULL *of* CRETE

 The WILD MARES *of* DIOMEDES

 HIPPOLYTE'S GOLDEN BELT

 KING.GERYON'S CATTLE

 The GOLDEN APPLES *of the* HESPERIDES

CERBERUS *the* HOUND *from* HADES

SPAIN

The Pillars
of Hercules